What the Army Needs to Know to Align Its Operational and Institutional Activities

Executive Summary

Frank Camm, Cynthia R. Cook, Ralph Masi, Anny Wong

Prepared for the United States Army

ARROYO CENTER

The research described in this report was sponsored by the United States Army under Contract No. DASW01-01-C-0003.

Library of Congress Cataloging-in-Publication Data

Camm, Frank A., 1949–
    What the Army needs to know to align its operational and institutional activities / Frank Camm, Cynthia R. Cook, Ralph Masi, [et al.].
      p. cm.
    Includes bibliographical references.
    ISBN-13: 978-0-8330-4000-8 (pbk. : alk. paper)
    ISBN-13: 978-0-8330-4001-5 (pbk. : alk. paper)
    1. United States. Army—Reorganization. I. Cook, Cynthia R., 1965– II. Masi, Ralph. III. Title.

UA25.C26 2007
355.30973—dc22

2006028288

Published 2007 by the RAND Corporation
1776 Main Street, P.O. Box 2138, Santa Monica, CA 90407-2138
1200 South Hayes Street, Arlington, VA 22202-5050
4570 Fifth Avenue, Suite 600, Pittsburgh, PA 15213-2665
RAND URL: http://www.rand.org/
To order RAND documents or to obtain additional information, contact
Distribution Services: Telephone: (310) 451-7002;
Fax: (310) 451-6915; Email: order@rand.org

Preface

This monograph is the executive summary for MG-530-A, written by Frank Camm, Cynthia R. Cook, Ralph Masi, and Anny Wong, and titled *What the Army Needs to Know to Align Its Operational and Institutional Activities.* These two documents were produced as part of a project called Adapting the Institutional U.S. Army to the Emerging Operating Force for the Office of the Deputy Chief of Staff for Operations and Plans (ODCSOPS, G-3). The study presents a way to define the expectations of the U.S. Army leadership about future performance in the institutional Army.

This project is the final product of an unusually long series of discussions with senior Army leaders. These discussions began in March 2004, when GEN George W. Casey, Jr., then–Vice Chief of Staff of the Army, asked the RAND Corporation to help him understand what outputs the institutional Army produced and how all the resources and activities in the institutional Army could be associated with these outputs. Transformation of the Army's operating force was well under way. A plan for major change would become public when the Army Campaign Plan (ACP) was published in May 2004. General Casey believed that a better understanding of the institutional Army would help the leadership determine how it would have to change to support the ongoing and anticipated changes in the operating force.

RAND's discussion with General Casey led, following his departure for Iraq, to an extended series of discussions, through the summer of 2004, with LTG James J. Lovelace, then–Director of the Army Staff. General Lovelace was working with members of the Army Science

Board on specific ways to reorganize the institutional Army and hoped that RAND could support that effort and the Office of Institutional Army Adaptation (OIAA) that would stand up shortly under his leadership. RAND's discussions with General Lovelace led to a focus on institutional "functions" that specifically support the operating force. General Lovelace asked RAND to determine what these functions should look like when the changes contemplated in the Army Campaign Plan were complete. RAND proposed to develop a method that Headquarters, Department of the Army (HQDA) could use to choose high-level performance metrics that specify what the major commands responsible for institutional activities should emphasize in their change efforts.

After long discussions within HQDA, the responsibility for overseeing the adaptation of the institutional Army to the emerging operating force and, as part of that, the new OIAA finally fell to MG David C. Ralston, Director of Force Management in ODCSOPS, G-3. In November 2004, General Ralston initiated the study that led to this monograph. He asked RAND to (1) develop a system of choosing performance metrics that senior Army leaders could use to specify what level of performance institutional activities should provide at any future point in time and to (2) focus on the institutional activities of greatest and most immediate importance to the operating force. For specificity, we agreed to focus on performance in the year at the end of the Program Objective Memorandum cycle then in play, 2013. General Ralston asked RAND to work closely with the OIAA as this work went forward. As the OIAA narrowed its focus to a set of initiatives to offer as near-term changes in the ACP during the winter and spring of 2005, General Ralston asked RAND to maintain its broader, longer-term view of the institutional Army. Our study maintains that broader view, illustrating how the Army could develop performance metrics for all the institutional activities highlighted in the ACP with examples focused on three of them.

This long path to choosing a specific set of questions for RAND to answer illustrates the profound challenge that the Army leadership faces in its ongoing efforts to improve alignment of the operational and institutional portions of the Army. Choosing the right question to ask is often a significant step toward developing an answer that will yield useful policy outcomes. The leadership took a long time to clarify its question to RAND precisely because it has had so little experience making specific decisions about links between the operational and institutional parts of the Army.

This work should interest policy analysts and decisionmakers concerned with (1) the relationship between the institutional activities—the tail—of a military organization and its operational activities—its teeth—and (2) how performance metrics for institutional activities can clarify expectations in that relationship. These metrics help clarify the notion that the institutional activities of a military organization are critical to the success of its operational activities and cannot be viewed, as they so often are, simply as a bill payer for changes to enhance operational capability. More generally, this work should interest those who seek to link the outcomes of public policies to the resources used to produce these outputs through families of internally consistent metrics. The well-known balanced scorecard is an example of one way to do this. Our study uses a closely related method that describes high-level processes in the value chains that deliver outputs from institutional activities to operational activities. The value chains described here help clarify the challenges involved in this kind of effort.

This research has been conducted in RAND Arroyo Center's Strategy, Doctrine, and Resources Program. RAND Arroyo Center, part of the RAND Corporation, is a federally funded research and development center sponsored by the United States Army. Questions and comments regarding this research are welcome and should be directed to the leader of the research team, Frank Camm, at Frank_Camm@rand.org.

The Project Unique Identification Code (PUIC) for the project that produced this document is DAPRR05034.

For more information on RAND Arroyo Center, contact the Director of Operations (telephone 310-393-0411, extension 6419; FAX 310-451-6952; email Marcy_Agmon@rand.org), or visit Arroyo's Web site at http://www.rand.org/ard/.

Contents

Figures

Acknowledgments

GEN George W. Casey, Jr., then–Vice Chief of Staff, initiated the discussions between the Army and RAND Arroyo Center that led to this project. LTG James J. Lovelace, then–Director of the Army Staff, worked closely with us to clarify the Army leadership's priorities with regard to the institutional Army. MG David C. Ralston, Director of Force Management in ODCSOPS, G-3, finalized the project description that framed the content of this study. Clifton E. Dickey of ODCSOPS, G-3, sponsored the completion of this summary and the related monograph and provided valuable support in disseminating the findings within Headquarters, Department of the Army. COL Ricky Gibbs and other members of the OIAA provided useful insights as we coordinated our ongoing activities with theirs. We had invaluable discussions with Army personnel associated with the Army Campaign Plan, Strategic Readiness System, Total Army Analysis, Training and Doctrine (TRADOC) Futures Center, U.S. Army Manpower Analysis Agency, and the specific functional areas addressed here, including accessioning, force well-being, logistics services, medical services, mobilization and demobilization, personnel management, and the Rapid Equipping Force and Rapid Fielding Initiative. LTG Richard G. Trefry (Ret.) and his staff at the Army Force Management School shared their unique and deep knowledge of how key processes in the institutional Army run.

The work underlying this report involved an unusual degree of cooperation throughout RAND Arroyo Center. Thomas L. McNaugher initiated the project within RAND, supported it through its many incarnations, and played an active role in framing the language in these documents. Lauri Zeman oversaw the project as head of the Strategy, Doctrine, and Resources Program in RAND Arroyo Center. William M. (Mike) Hix, Henry A. (Chip) Leonard, and Tom McNaugher were actively involved in discussions with the Director of the Army Staff about how to frame this work. Mike Hix and Valerie Williams provided careful reviews of all the material in the final draft. Mike Hix, Chip Leonard, David Kassing, and Eric Peltz provided direct assistance to the OIAA on services, training, mobilization and demobilization, and logistics policy. Timothy Bonds and Nathan Tranquilli worked through Army manpower and personnel databases to help us scope the institutional Army. Carl J. Dahlman, Susan M. Gates, Victoria A. Greenfield, Mike Hix, Nancy Y. Moore, Albert A. Robbert, and Bernard D. Rostker provided valuable guidance on the input-output model described in Chapter Two. John A. Ausink (on force well-being), Gary Cecchine (medical), Rick Eden (logistics), Bryan W. Hallmark (training), Christopher E. Hanks (acquisition), Susan D. Hosek (medical), Leland Joe (acquisition), David E. Johnson (medical), Chip Leonard (training), Dave Kassing (mobilization and demobilization), and Eric Peltz (logistics) provided valuable institutional knowledge in their fields of expertise and helped us make relevant contacts in the Army. Victoria Greenfield and Valerie Williams shared their ongoing work on logic modeling and helped us appreciate insights from it relevant to the formal evaluation of value chains presented here. Katharine Watkins Webb provided useful information on ongoing changes in the planning, programming, budgeting, and execution system relevant to our work. Jerry Sollinger helped improve the presentation. We simply could not have executed a project covering such a broad range of topics without the active support of our Arroyo Center colleagues.

We thank all those who made it possible for us to produce this document and the related monograph, and we retain full responsibility for its accuracy and objectivity.

Abbreviations

ACP	Army Campaign Plan
APS	Army Posture Statement
DA	Department of the Army
DoD	Department of Defense
HQDA	Headquarters, Department of the Army
ODCSOPS	Office of the Deputy Chief of Staff for Operations and Plans
OIAA	Office of Institutional Army Adaptation
POM	Program Objective Memorandum
SMS	Strategic Management System
TRADOC	Training and Doctrine Command

CHAPTER ONE

Introduction

As the U.S. Army transforms its combat force, inevitably the institutional Army—the "generating force" that fills and sustains the Army's combat units—must change as well. Stabilizing soldiers at posts and in units demands different personnel and training routines from those that supported the Army's long-standing "individual-replacement" system. Developing and fielding an integrated "system of systems" and delivering it in sets to units entering the force generation cycle likewise calls for generating force activities markedly different from those mastered in years past. And of course a whole series of supporting organizations must adapt to the global deployments of an Army that will be based largely in the United States rather than overseas. Transformation of the institutional Army is surely as dramatic as the transformation of the Army's combat force.

Yet it is far less well understood. Over many years, the Army has developed an array of metrics to assess the performance of its combat units. Not surprisingly, the current Army Campaign Plan (ACP) and Army Posture Statement (APS) offer clear and fairly succinct visions for this part of the force: The Army seeks a more joint-oriented, expeditionary, modular, rebalanced, stabilized and brigade-based operating force. When these documents turn to the institutional Army, by contrast, they tell us, repeatedly, that the Army will use fewer resources to provide better support to the warfighter. It is an appealing thought, but such a concept raises a huge array of questions about how the institutional Army should change to provide that support. It also overlooks the possibility that some parts of the generating force may need more, rather than fewer, resources to perform crucial new tasks optimally.

The potential danger in this relative lack of keen understanding is that laudable efforts to enforce efficiency on the institutional Army will "improve" deeply ingrained but now misdirected processes or will reach elegant, but suboptimal, local solutions in terms of the Army's overall transformational goals. Needed is a method for aligning the operational and institutional portions of the Army for transformational purposes. This project, launched by then–Vice Chief of Staff GEN George Casey and sponsored by the Army's Office of the Deputy Chief of Staff for Operations and Plans (ODCSOPS, G-3), explains how to evaluate value chains to develop information that can promote such alignment. And it formally evaluates value chains to develop illustrative high-level performance metrics relevant to the alignment of institutional medical, enlisted accessioning, and short-term acquisition services to the operating force.

CHAPTER TWO

The Institutional Army and Its Place in the U.S. Army

The APS and ACP summarize senior leadership views of how the operational and institutional parts of the Army should change to implement transformation. In phrasing that echoes similar documents from years past, the APS and ACP direct the Army to increase its operational capabilities by (1) shifting resources from institutional to operational activities and, at the same time, (2) changing its institutional activities in ways that improve support of operational forces. To understand what such "realignment" means in a bit more detail, it helps to present the resource environment in which the Army's institutional activities support its operating forces. The institutional Army includes a wide variety of activities that, roughly speaking, all fall into one of four categories:

- *creation, integration, and oversight* of the Army as a whole, including the operating forces
- accessing, training, and sustainment of *personnel assets*
- design, procurement, and sustainment of *materiel and information assets*
- *direct, global* delivery of logistics, medical, installation, mobilization, and information *support services* to users inside and outside the institutional Army, including operational forces.

Each institutional activity converts inputs, in the form of dollars and personnel services, into outputs that the institutional Army then delivers to the operational Army and to a number of nonoperational users, including dependents, retirees, civil works, and local communities. In this setting, "outputs" are goods and services that can be explicitly defined in terms that are relevant to user priorities. For example, institutional medical activities do not deliver vaccinations or surgeries to the operating force; rather, they deliver well soldiers.[1] Within fixed constraints on the Army's dollar budget and its military end strength, any realignment must change how institutional activities use dollars and personnel to support operational and nonoperational users.

In effect, realignment changes the balance of interests among two kinds of stakeholders outside the institutional Army:

- representatives of various operational and nonoperational user priorities
- resource stewards that allocate fixed numbers of dollars and personnel hours among competing efforts to (1) produce outputs from existing processes in institutional activities or (2) invest in changing these processes.

Several resource stewards play important roles in the Department of Army (DA). The Office of the Deputy Chief of the Army for Programs (G-8) and the Comptroller are, of course, responsible for the allocation of the Army's dollar budget, both in the near term and over the planning period. The Army's G-3 oversees the Army's allocation of its military end-strength ceiling. And a more diffuse set of players attempts to protect dollars and personnel from the demands of immediate priorities so that the Army can apply them to improve processes in the operational and institutional parts of the Army. In effect, these resource stewards are responsible for the resources under their control and must release them to any institutional or operational activities as an integral part of alignment.

High-level Army guidance is not specific about which operational user priorities are relevant to realignment between the operational and

---

[1] Vaccinations and surgeries are two among many tasks that institutional activities perform to generate well soldiers. Operators do not care about the details of these tasks; they care about soldiers' readiness for military service. Therefore, we define the outputs of institutional medical activities as soldiers who are well enough to perform their military duties.

institutional Army. The Army currently thinks about operational capability, for example, in four qualitatively different ways:

1. At a high policy level, the APS and ACP speak of jointness, modularity, force balance, expeditionary capability, and brigade focus.
2. In broad conceptual terms, Army planners and analysts speak of the lethality, deployability, survivability, agility, sustainability, and so on of a deployed force.
3. In force planning, through the Total Army Analysis process, the Army leadership speaks of the level of risk associated with the Army's ability to execute the missions assigned to it in the Joint Program Guidance.
4. In operations, commanders speak of the readiness of their personnel, materiel, and information assets relative to stated requirements.

Each perspective offers a potential entry point for explaining how a change in the institutional Army might improve operational capability. High-level Army guidance does not explicitly state that increasing the level of certain institutional activities that provide direct support to the operating force is likely the best way to rebalance the priorities of the stakeholders outside the institutional Army that are relevant to the institutional Army in ways that increase operational capability. This is one way to emphasize that the senior leadership's desire to reduce the size of the institutional Army does not lead to a reduction in all institutional activities. In fact, when we change the balance of priorities among relevant stakeholders outside the institutional Army, it is impossible to look at individual institutional activities in isolation. Realignment will succeed only if the Army leadership learns how to link each institutional activity to the broader context in which it allocates its limited resources across the Army. Effective alignment of the institutional and operational portions of the Army means specifying this link in terms that are concrete enough to guide particular resource changes within the institutional Army.

Figure 2.1 brings together in a single diagram the points discussed previously. The "stewards" box summarizes the kinds of Army organizations that allocate authorizations for dollars and military personnel. The "institutional" box lists four qualitatively different kinds of activities that occur in the institutional Army. The "operational" box highlights four ways to talk about operational priorities relevant to institutional activities. The "nonoperational" box highlights the users other than the operating force that the institutional Army supports. The flow from resource inputs through institutional activities to institutional outputs and policy outcomes ties these boxes together. Authorizations for dollars and military personnel flow into the Army, where DA-level

Figure 2.1
Relationships Relevant to Alignment of Institutional Activities

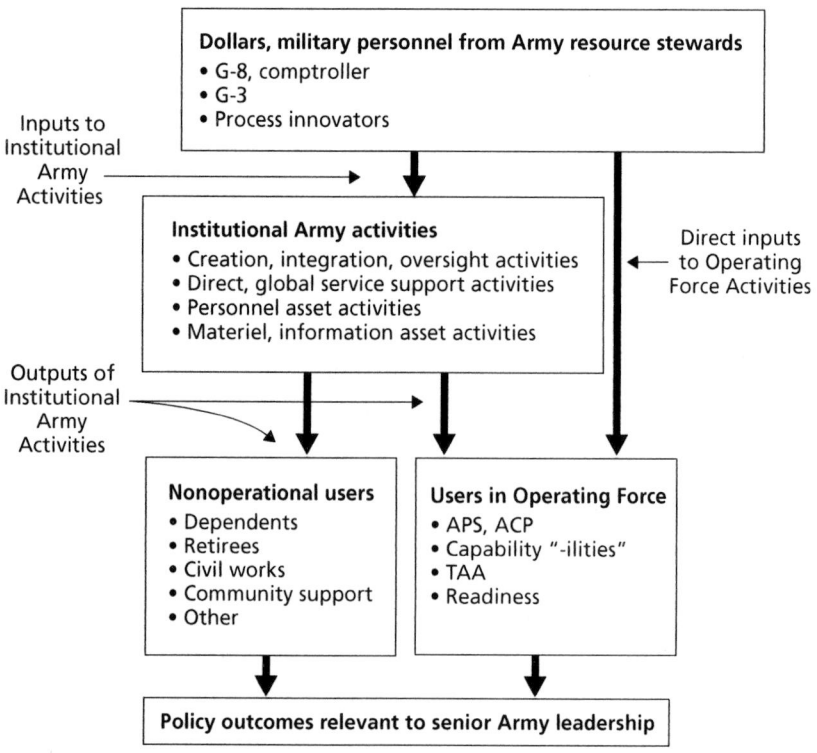

resource stewards allocate these inputs to operational and institutional portions of the Army. The activities in the institutional Army convert the resource inputs they receive into institutional outputs that they then deliver to external operational and nonoperational users. These users apply the institutional outputs they receive in ways that affect policy outcomes relevant to the senior leadership of the Army. The contents of the boxes highlight topics that this monograph addresses in greater detail. Effective alignment of institutional and operational portions of the Army "appropriately balances" the priorities of the resource stewards that align dollar and personnel authorizations with the priorities of operational and nonoperational users of outputs from institutional activities. Resource stewards and users of institutional outputs seek to balance their priorities in ways that promote policy outcomes desired by the senior Army leadership.

CHAPTER THREE

The Information Requirements of Effective Alignment

Ongoing efforts to transform the Army presumably seek to change the balance among the interests of the stakeholders described above in ways that promote outcomes that senior Army leaders seek to achieve in the new, ever-unfolding political-military environment in which they operate. What information does the Army leadership need to coordinate this change? In our setting, information about where institutional activities touch the rest of the Army is important. Figure 3.1 highlights four "touch points" where institutional activities (A) deliver outputs to operational activities, (B) deliver outputs to nonoperational activities, (C) draw resources from Army-wide resource stewards, and (D) change their internal processes in ways that could impose transitional effects at one of the other three touch points. Information likely to be relevant at each touch point includes answers to the following kinds of questions:

A. What outputs does each institutional activity produce and deliver to the operating force? What attributes of these outputs are relevant to operational capability? How does a change in each attribute affect operational capability?
B. What are the answers to these questions for institutional outputs delivered to users outside the operational Army?
C. Given the dollars and military personnel the Army has available to allocate over its planning period, what level of operational capability can it realistically expect to achieve by the end of that planning horizon? What allocation of dollars and military personnel does this entail between the operational and institutional parts of the Army?

D. What process changes can each institutional activity make to enhance the attributes of its outputs that increase operational capability? What operational improvements will each of these institutional process changes effect? When? How much will each change cost? What allocation of dollars and military personnel does this entail between using institutional processes to produce current output and improving these processes?

The leadership's understanding of the answers to these questions may depend on professional military judgment or on detailed empirical data. Without such an understanding, the Army leadership cannot predict how reallocating the resources available to it will affect operational capability. It can observe the level of operational capability it achieves at any point in time. But it cannot know whether it can do

Figure 3.1
Information Requirements of Effective Alignment

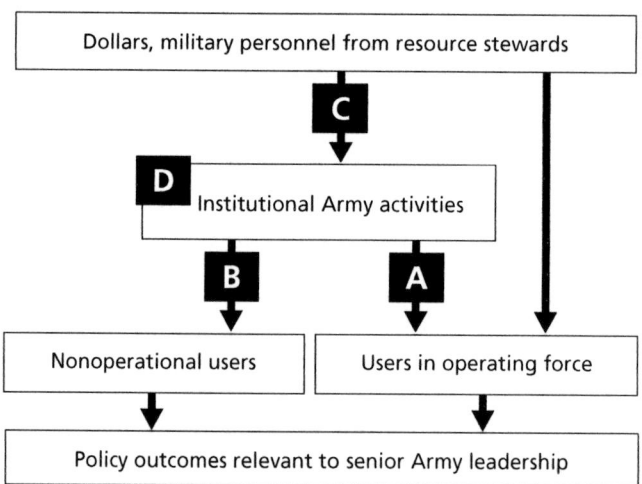

A. Attributes of institutional outputs and how they affect the operating force
B. Attributes of institutional outputs and how they affect other users
C. Institutional resource requirements to achieve stated operational outcomes
D. Characteristics of initiatives to improve institutional processes

RAND *MG530/1-3.1*

better with the resources at hand or how it might do better. The sounder the information the leadership has to develop answers to the questions above, the more effective it can be at aligning institutional activities to the operating force in ways that improve operational capability. Our analysis strongly suggests that evaluation of value chains can provide the kinds of information Army leaders need to make the most informed decisions possible.

CHAPTER FOUR

Evaluating Value Chains to Support Effective Alignment

Formal evaluation of value chains links policy *outcomes* to the government *resources* needed to produce them. It develops a consensus set of qualitative beliefs about how a value chain converts the *resources* that an agency consumes into agency *outputs* and then converts these outputs into policy *outcomes*. In our setting, evaluating value chains can use qualitative beliefs about the value chain to relate dollars and military personnel to the outputs of an institutional activity and then relate these outputs into operational capability outcomes. Some of the resources consumed directly produce current institutional outputs. Others are invested in process improvement to increase the institutional activity's ability to produce outputs in the future. The more precise beliefs are and the more carefully they are validated against real-world experience, the better. But the relationships in question are so complex that the Army must be prepared to start with simple sets of shared beliefs. As it learns where better information will add the most value, it can collect and analyze data to sharpen and validate these beliefs.

This basic approach provides a simple architecture for developing metrics that the Army can use to answer the four sets of questions above. Using shared beliefs about relationships among inputs, outputs, and outcomes as a guide, it first clarifies goals for operational capabilities and then uses them to derive goals for institutional outputs and finally goals for resource inputs. These cascaded goals provide the basis for choosing metrics that the leadership can use to coordinate change. Figure 4.1 summarizes these points. The flow diagram in the middle

Figure 4.1
Generic Value Chain That Aligns the Operating Force and Institutional Army

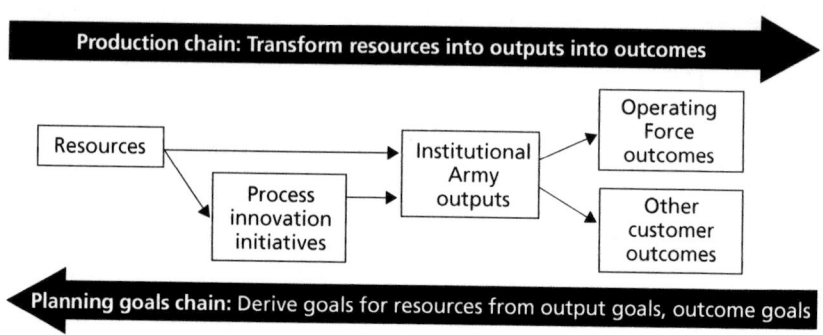

illustrates a "production chain" derived from subjective beliefs about the relationships shown in Figure 2.1. This production chain provides the basis for defining a corresponding "planning goals chain." Transforming goals for outcomes, outputs, and resources into terms that the Army can measure and track defines a set of performance metrics the Army can use to clarify the leadership's expectations about the alignment of its operational and institutional activities.

In particular, when assessing any specific institutional activity, our evaluation of the relevant value chains seeks the answers to four kinds of questions:

1. Who are the specific *stakeholders* outside the institutional Army that must agree on a plan that balances outcomes for users with inputs consumed by the institutional Army? What do they care about?

2. What specific *attributes of institutional outputs* do they care about? What metrics can the Army use to measure these attributes in a way that all relevant stakeholders understand?

3. What specific *improvements in attributes* of institutional outputs are feasible to pursue? How long will they take? What will they cost?

4. What specific *resources*—numbers of dollars and military personnel—must the Army allocate to the institutional Army to achieve any desired level of institutional output attributes?

Formal evaluation of a value chain offers a rigorous, disciplined way to develop metrics that the Army can use to discuss these questions, reach high-level agreement on them, and track progress relative to any set of answers agreed to. Our report applies value chain evaluation to develop illustrative sets of metrics relevant to three of the four categories of institutional Army activities described above—personnel assets; materiel and information assets; and global, end-to-end service support.

To illustrate here how we developed and applied answers to the four sets of questions above, we present the elements of the model of the value chain we developed for activities related to materiel and information assets, based on short-term acquisition. This is the simplest of the three models of value chains that we developed here.

Short-term acquisition rapidly meets new materiel challenges and addresses technological challenges that emerge during a deployment. It uses high-level focus and integration to accelerate existing acquisition processes and to develop solutions to problems in an operational setting. Consider the four sets of questions in turn.

Who are the relevant *stakeholders*? Three sets of Army stakeholders outside the institutional Army are important to short-term acquisition:[1]

- *Unit commanders and soldiers.* Unit commanders care about the ability of their soldiers to function effectively. The soldiers want

---

[1] Of course, other interested stakeholders exist outside the Army, including civilian and military leaders of the Department of Defense (DoD) who oversee the Army and integrate it into a joint force, the Office of Management and Budget, and members of Congress. Even as DoD moves toward greater joint integration, design and oversight of Army institutional activities remain responsibilities of the Army leadership. In their roles as stakeholders in short-term acquisition, the Army leaders named here bring to bear the interests of other interested stakeholders external to the Army.

to avoid buying mission-related items that the Army can get for them through short-term acquisition.

- *Resource stewards.* G-3 monitors the requirements for military personnel generated by short-term acquisition. G-8 and the Comptroller monitor the requirements for dollars.
- *Others.* The Vice Chief of Staff uses his personal authority to make short-term acquisition work and justifies that application of his limited leadership resources by verifying that the activity has sufficient demonstrable effects on deployed force capability. The Secretary and Chief of Staff of the Army monitor short-term acquisition for ideas on how to transform acquisition as a whole.

What *output attributes* do these stakeholders care about? Stakeholders can benefit from metrics that assess how well short-term acquisition operates relative to their goals. Their goals can be framed in terms of such output attributes as the following: speed or responsiveness of acquisition, effect on operational mission performance, effect on risk to the mission or soldier, effect on soldier purchases of mission-related materiel, cost-effectiveness of the acquisition process itself, and degree to which new ideas migrate from short-term acquisition to other acquisition activities. Metrics can be developed for each of these. Speed and responsiveness, for example, can be measured, in this context, in a variety of ways, including the following: percentage of a unit's kit filled when it deploys, percentage of kit available at some stated last acceptable date, or number of days required to provide newly identified items.

Looking across all institutional activities, stakeholders outside the institutional Army tend to emphasize specific elements of four types of attributes of an institutional output: throughput capacity, quality, speed or responsiveness, and resource costs. Throughput measures the rate at which an institutional activity can deliver output—for example, number of battalions mobilized, number of individuals trained, or number of tons transported per period of time.

Quality rises when the match improves between what the operating force wants and what an institutional activity delivers when it delivers an output. Quality rises, for example, as the match between skills demanded and skills delivered increases, reliability of repair increases, or the match increases between the schedule demanded for delivery and the schedule met in delivery. Speed and responsiveness are elements of quality that receive so much attention today that we have broken them out. Speed increases as the time between an operational request and an institutional delivery falls. Responsiveness increases as an institutional activity's ability to change direction in the face of new operational priorities increases—in terms of calendar time or match between new requirements and delivered capabilities.

Costs increase as the operating force must commit more of its own resources to accept an output from an institutional activity. For example, if an institutional logistics activity improves how it packages items shipped to theater, operational units can cut their costs by using fewer man-hours to accept, sort, and deliver the items to recipients in theater. If a working capital fund institutional activity reduces the price it charges for items it delivers to the operating force, the operating force faces lower costs, because a given operations and maintenance budget can now buy more from the institutional Army.

What *process improvements* could affect output attributes relevant to these stakeholders? A variety of process changes could potentially improve the performance of short-term acquisition relative to attributes that its stakeholders care about. For example, the use of Web pages could simplify the process of choosing candidate items to acquire rapidly, affecting mission performance and solders' need to buy their own equipment. Selection of prequalified sources could speed execution of materiel and research and development services, improve the quality of services delivered, and reduce costs. The standard metrics used in current acquisition programs can be used to measure and track progress toward goals on performance (that is, how an improvement changes an attribute relevant to a stakeholder), schedule, and cost.

What *resources* does the activity consume? Short-term acquisition consumes very few military personnel but large sums of money. The Rapid Fielding Initiative, for example, spent $991 million in fiscal year 2005. Some of these dollars and personnel are consumed in clearly identified activities and can be fairly easily tracked. The institutional Army consumes others in supporting activities—such as installation, logistics, information, personnel, and business—that do not charge short-term acquisition activities for their services. The dollars and personnel consumed in these activities should be allocated to the institutional outputs that they support. Doing this in the Rapid Equipping Force, another element of short-term acquisition, is a special challenge, because so much of this activity involves expediting and integrating materiel testing and procurement activities in Army activities not primarily identified with short-term acquisition. The dollars and personnel consumed in these expedited and integrated activities should be allocated to short-term acquisition.

Similar resource issues arise in any institutional activity the Army wants to align to the operating force. The Army currently has a very limited ability to associate military dollar and personnel costs with specific institutional outputs. When an activity produces more than one important output—for example, training of military doctors and direct medical support of a deployed force—the Army has no well-defined way to allocate the resources that the institutional activity consumes directly among these outputs. When institutional activity A—for example, a combat training center—receives inputs from institutional activity B—for example, acquisition of weapon systems—without paying for them, the Army has no well-defined way to allocate the resources that activity B consumes to the outputs that activity A delivers to the operating force. If the Army were to shift specific training responsibilities from institutional schoolhouses to operational units, the Army could not easily predict the effect of the change on institutional or operational demands for dollars or military billets (much less the real readiness of operational units).

CHAPTER FIVE

The Way Forward for Policy

Using metrics to improve the performance of the institutional Army is not a new idea. It is closely related to two other Army initiatives currently under way. But the way we derive metrics from a set of shared subjective beliefs about a value chain provides a way to move beyond these initiatives in important ways.

Expand the Strategic Management System to Capture Alignment Targets

The Army Strategic Management System (SMS) is developing a hierarchical suite of metrics that, as it is implemented and used to support decisionmaking, could help align policy and resource decisions throughout the Army to the priorities of the leadership. As a version of a balanced scorecard, that is what the SMS is supposed to do. Elements of the approach to evaluating value chains described above closely parallel the four perspectives highlighted in a balanced scorecard. Operating force performance is one *user* perspective. Delivery of institutional outputs is an *internal process* perspective. Institutional process improvement is a *growth and learning* perspective. And institutional resource requirements constitute a *resource* perspective.

The metrics relevant to the alignment of the operational and institutional portions of the Army could, in effect, constitute the portion of a balanced scorecard that looks forward to a desired future level of performance. As the SMS expands its focus from current readiness to planning, the metrics described here could become an integral part of the SMS. For now, because they focus on the benefits and costs of process change, the metrics described here differ qualitatively from those in the current SMS, which mainly focus on the performance of existing Army processes relative to current performance targets.

Place Institutional Lean Six Sigma Initiatives in a Broader Operational Context

Lean Six Sigma initiatives throughout the Army are developing ways to make individual processes better, faster, and cheaper. Because these initiatives are designed and implemented locally, they tend to focus on performance metrics relevant to individual local processes. For example, a depot-level maintenance initiative might release resources to the operating force by increasing the utilization rate of depot maintenance assets. Such an initiative could also inadvertently reduce overall support to deployed forces by increasing customer wait times—a performance factor potentially beyond the scope of the local depot initiative. By explicitly cascading performance priorities from the operating force, the approach to evaluating value chains described above seeks a system view that would discourage such dysfunctional local process "improvements."

In effect, the evaluation of value chains can provide a higher-level context in which to frame Lean Six Sigma initiatives, which can then pursue Army-wide goals at the local level. Value-chain evaluation also generates higher-level information that the Army leadership can use to understand how parts of the institutional Army fit together and hence how reallocations of resources among local institutional processes might affect operational capability. Lean Six Sigma tends to focus inside local processes and is not typically used to improve allocation of resources across separable processes.

Develop Better Empirically Based Information Relevant to Alignment

Because the approach to evaluating value chains described above looks beyond current Army initiatives, it underscores the desirability of additional, empirically based information that existing Army methods and processes currently cannot generate. Some examples of particular importance include the following:

- *The total dollars and military personnel that the institutional Army requires to produce specific levels of institutional outputs with specific attributes.* Formal evaluation of value chains could frame the application of activity-based costing to ensure that it addresses the questions relevant to alignment.
- *Specific operational goals beyond the first few years of the Future Years Defense Program that can be used to motivate and prioritize investment in specific initiatives to improve processes within institutional activities.* Currently, individual institutional initiatives typically do not flow from specific future desired operational outcomes that the Army leadership could use to compare them, choose among them, and maintain accountability for results.
- *Broadly understood qualitative assessment of the quality of specific institutional outputs delivered to the operating force.* The Army currently lacks a broadly shared qualitative language that operators and institutional leaders could use to characterize goals for quality and to sustain accountability against these goals.
- *Well-defined information on how changes in specific attributes of institutional outputs affect specific aspects of operational capability.* Today, the Army typically relies much more heavily on professional military judgment than on empirical evidence to assess the likely operational usefulness of specific changes in institutional outputs.

- *Broad agreement on how the versions of operational capability described above—the four that focus on high-level policy, broad performance concept, mission risk, and readiness—relate to one another and so how to trade off among institutional outputs whose effects on the operating force the senior leaders understand in terms of different versions of operational capability.* If leaders use, say, personnel readiness to characterize the operational effects on one institutional change (e.g., the number of accessions delivered per period) and, say, mission risk to characterize the operational effects of another institutional change (e.g., the personal characteristics of recruits or the content of the training that recruits receive) but do not agree on how personnel readiness relates to mission risk, then it becomes difficult to align goals within the operating force, much less goals in the operational and institutional parts of the Army.

As noted above, the Army can continue to rely on professional military judgment to provide the information it needs to reallocate resources in ways that improve the alignment of the operating and institutional parts of the Army. But the better the information described in the bullet points above, the better able the Army will be to reallocate resources in ways that promote the long-term goals of operational transformation. The leadership must decide how much it wants to invest in improving this kind of information. Formal evaluation of value chains can help the Army determine where it is likely to be cost-effective to invest in methods and processes that can generate better, empirically based metrics. Alignment should improve as the information used to frame it improves. But the Army clearly has to weigh the value of refined alignment against the costs of collecting the information required to allow such refinement.